T0194751

TRUTH
THAT BRINGS
PEACE,
LOVE,
JOY
AND
HOPE

JERRY GASPARD

WESTBOW
PRESS®
A DIVISION OF THOMAS NELSON
& ZONDERVAN

Scripture quotations marked (NLT) are taken from the Holy
Bible, New Living Translation, copyright © 1996, 2004, 2007 by
Tyndale House Foundation. Used by permission of Tyndale House
Publishers, Inc., Carol Stream, Illinois 60188. All rights reserved.

THE HOLY BIBLE, NEW INTERNATIONAL VERSION®,
NIV® Copyright © 1973, 1978, 1984, 2011 by Biblica, Inc.®
Used by permission. All rights reserved worldwide.

WestBow Press books may be ordered through booksellers or by contacting:

WestBow Press
A Division of Thomas Nelson & Zondervan
1663 Liberty Drive
Bloomington, IN 47403
www.westbowpress.com
1 (866) 928-1240

Because of the dynamic nature of the Internet, any web addresses or
links contained in this book may have changed since publication and
may no longer be valid. The views expressed in this work are solely those
of the author and do not necessarily reflect the views of the publisher,
and the publisher hereby disclaims any responsibility for them.

Any people depicted in stock imagery provided by Thinkstock are models,
and such images are being used for illustrative purposes only.
Certain stock imagery © Thinkstock.

ISBN: 978-1-9736-1494-4 (sc)
ISBN: 978-1-9736-1493-7 (e)

Library of Congress Control Number: 2018900488

Print information available on the last page.

WestBow Press rev. date: 01/23/2018

CONTENTS

INTRODUCTION

The Bible is God's truth, and he cannot lie. God's word is his will for your life.

God wants you to enjoy your life and have an intimate relationship with him and his Son, Jesus Christ. All of God's promises are for you to have: victory, success, love, joy, hope, patience, kindness, peace, faithfulness, gentleness, self-control, and a sound mind. It is for those who obey God and his son, Jesus Christ.

In Jesus Christ, you have life and life more abundantly. You serve a God who is more than enough. God does not want you to barely get by. He wants to bless you, so you can be a blessing to others. Jesus is the truth and the life. In Christ, you will know the truth, and the truth will set you free.

God has given me the assignment of writing this book, with the help of the Holy Spirit, to reach out to all Christians and those who have yet to receive Jesus as their Lord and Savior. I pray that as you read this book, God will give you a revelation of who he is and show you his great love for you.

CHAPTER 1

God's Protection

God's protection is for those who have yet to be saved and for those who are saved. God assigns a guardian angel to watch over you and protect you. I would like to share with you my testimony of God's grace and protection.

I should have died three times in my life. When I was a teenager and working to save for college expenses, I got a summer job working on a pipeline barge in an offshore oil field. It was quite fascinating to see how a pipeline was laid on the ocean floor. At the front of the barge, about ten feet above sea level, the assembly line for welding the pipeline began. The pipe would vary in size according to the specification of the oil company; it was usually twenty- to thirty-six-inch pipe. Sections of pipe were approximately ten feet long, and they had a two-inch concrete coating. The sections had one foot of bare steel exposed on both ends, and they would be loaded onto a rolling rack that rolled the pipe onto the first welding stall.

There were five welding stalls along the way downward.

The pipe would be welded and buffed at each station as it descended toward sea level. I worked at the sixth station, where the pipes were sealed. We would strap a sheet of steel tin around the exposed pipe and cut an open flap, and then a very hot mixture of tar and sand would be poured to fill the exposed pipe. The flap would be strapped and sealed and sent on to a one-hundred-foot pontoon; the pipe would then be laid gently onto the ocean floor.

The sea could be as calm as glass or as rough as fifteen-foot waves. Our station was about three feet above sea level. One day, we were working in twelve- to fifteen-foot seas. I was wearing a long-sleeved denim shirt, blue jeans, and heavy-duty work boots, which made it very difficult, if not impossible, to swim. A fifteen-foot wave came over me and sucked me into the ocean. As I fell back into the ocean, I began sinking. While underwater, I could feel someone grabbing my hand and placing it on a ladder that was on the side of the barge. It was my guardian angel. I was able to climb aboard the barge. I should have drowned, but God had better plans for me.

On another occasion while I was in college, I had a sinus infection and went home for the weekend. I was taking antibiotics and decided to go out for a drink or two. I had one beer and decided to go home. On my way home, I felt really sleepy. About one-fourth of a mile from my home, I fell asleep going about sixty miles per hour. As I rounded a curve, I drove head on into a ditch culvert. To my amazement, I had totaled my father's truck yet walked away unharmed (and I was not wearing a seatbelt). God's guardian angel protected me again. Death denied a second time.

My third brush with death began on a Sunday morning

in February 2006. I had just attended church with my wife and daughter. As we were heading home, I had to turn left at a traffic light. I was in the left-hand turn lane at a red light. It was a beautiful, crisp sunny day with a clear blue sky, when all of a sudden a driver in a pickup truck struck me from behind. The driver had fallen asleep. I suffered a torn disc from the collision.

A spinal disc is made out of a jellylike substance that acts like a shock absorber between the vertebrae. When the disc is torn, it releases toxins onto the surrounding nerves, which can be extremely painful. I went to a pain management doctor, who prescribed Lortab for my pain. As the pain grew worse, I was advised to see a neurosurgeon for surgery. I made the appointment, and we decided surgery was needed to repair the disc. About two weeks before my operation, however, my health insurance company called to say they would not pay for the surgery. Apparently, the company thought this type of surgery did not have a good success rate.

I was devastated; my only option was to live on pain medications. The pain continued to increase, so my doctor prescribed heavier dosages. Over time, I became addicted to the pain medication. Eventually, I had a mental breakdown from bipolar disorder and was hospitalized six different times. I suffered from severe depression and was delusional.

I remember gazing at the sun one day, when I saw the sun expand until it split into two and became two suns. I know this was not possible, but my eyes were seeing things differently. I also began to hear voices in my mind that would hinder rational thinking. On one occasion, the voice told me I needed to go to a mountain to hear from God, like Moses did. The next day, I started my journey to Colorado. I ended up in Durango. I stayed overnight in a small rundown hotel. I heard a strange voice in my mind telling me that my vehicle would be stolen. Well, I thought if my truck was going to be stolen, I would make it easy for them. So I left the keys in the ignition. I felt a demonic presence in that place. God's grace intervened, and my truck was still there the next morning.

I packed up and decided to return home. On my way back on the interstate, out of nowhere, an eighteen-wheeler appeared, almost on my bumper. I sped up, and he sped up. I thought the devil was trying to kill me. I floored the gas pedal all the way down to get away. I cruised at ninety-five miles per hour until I approached Denver. A voice told me to follow a green car ahead of me, so I did. The voice then told me to follow an eighteen-wheeler and not to lose it. It was snowing heavily at this time, and visibility was low. The eighteen-wheeler pulled into a truck stop and refueled. I went over to the driver and asked where our next stop was. He looked at me as if I were crazy—but I really was.

I had to go to the restroom, and when I returned, the eighteen-wheeler was gone. Another voice told me to keep on driving and take my seatbelt off, so I did. I remember driving around ninety miles per hour in the snowstorm, with limited visibility, when suddenly a sharp curve was ahead of me that I did not see. I drove off the mountainous road and was airborne. I could not see where I was headed; I felt my guardian angel restrain me before impact. I landed in a concrete drainage canal with about a foot of mud. I emerged from the wreckage with only three fractured ribs. A police officer attending the scene told me it was not possible to live through such a crash.

God works in ways we cannot understand. God was not

ready for me to die; my destiny had not been fulfilled. God rescues the godly from danger (Proverbs 11:8 NLT).

I still struggled with bipolar depression. My marriage had crumbled because of my unpredictability, lack of self-worth, hopelessness, and despair. I did not love myself, so how was I to love my wife? When no one showed up to pick me up from the mental hospital, I felt rejection. The deepest pain is when someone close to you rejects you.

I spent over two years out of my right mind. I was destitute, depressed, lonely, and hopeless, with no direction, and I lacked a desire to live. I didn't have a reason to get out of bed. After two years had passed, God sent me to a psychiatrist who was able to put me on the right medication to correct the chemical imbalance in my brain. God can work through doctors and medicine. As a result, I was able to think clearly and be my old self again.

Although I had lost hope and my faith had failed me, God was merciful and restored my faith. I began to read and study the Bible. Then I read books about positive thinking. The scriptures tell us that we become what we think. If you think success, you will get success. If you think defeat, you will find defeat.

God will command his angels concerning you to guard you in all your ways (Psalm 91:11 NLT). Angels are ministering spirits to care for those who will receive salvation (Hebrews 1:14 NLT). Fear of the Lord gives life, security, and protection from harm (Proverbs 19:23 NLT). The Lord watches over those who fear him and over those who rely on his unfailing love (Psalm 33:18 NLT).

CHAPTER 2

God Loves You

The greatest desire that humans have is to be loved and accepted. God has placed that desire in us so we can turn to his unconditional love and acceptance. Because of sin, we do not have fellowship with God. But he has a plan to redeem us and bring us back to him. In his wisdom, God sent his Son, Jesus, as a sacrifice for our sins. Jesus endured the same hardships, temptations, discrimination, rejection, persecution, and suffering that we humans go through in life. Jesus paid the ultimate price for the forgiveness of our sins and redemption with God by shedding his blood on the cross. In Jesus, we have redemption and the forgiveness of sins through his blood (Ephesians 1:7 NLT). God's plan has always been to adopt us into his own family by bringing us to himself through Jesus Christ (Ephesians 1:15 NLT).

God has purchased our freedom with his blood and has forgiven all our sins (Colossians 1:14 NLT). God tells us to love the Lord your God with all your heart, with all your soul, and with all your strength (Deuteronomy 6:5 NLT).

Taste and see that the Lord is good; blessed is the one who takes refuge in him (Psalm 34:8 NIV).

The Lord is a good refuge in time of trouble. He cares for those who trust in him (Nahum 1:7 NIV). God's love for us is great. Love is patient and kind. Love is not jealous or boastful or proud or rude. Love does not demand its own way. Love is not irritable and keeps no record of when it is wronged. It is never glad about injustice but rejoices whenever the truth wins out. Love never gives up, never loses faith, is always hopeful, and endures through every circumstance. Love will last forever (1 Corinthians 13:4–8 NLT). This is the kind of love God wants us to have.

These characteristics are not automatic when you become a Christian. It will take time, endurance through trials and tribulations, and testing of your faith to help you grow into maturity. Know this: God loves you so much that he sacrificed his Son for the forgiveness of your sins, so that you would turn from your sinful nature and turn to him for your salvation and restoration. While we were sinners, God loved us. He draws us to him with his unconditional love. Because of God's great love for us, he is rich in mercy (Ephesians 2:4 NIV).

Once we receive salvation, God calls us his children (Luke 10:20 NIV). We are known as Christians by our love for others. The angels in heaven rejoice when a sinner repents and accepts Jesus as his Lord and Savior. Jesus promises that those who are his will not be lost. The Kingdom of God is within you: righteousness, joy, and peace in the Holy Spirit.

God destroyed sin's control over us by giving his Son (Jesus) as a sacrifice for our sins (Romans 8:3 NLT). The

Lord is wonderfully good to those who wait for him and seek him (Lamentations 3:25 NLT). God is love, and all who live in love live in God, and God lives in them (1 John 4:16 NLT).

CHAPTER 3

God's Plan for Salvation

S alvation equals eternal life in heaven. God has a plan for your salvation which is revealed in the Holy Scriptures.

For God so loved the world he gave his only Son, so that everyone who believes in him will not perish but have eternal life (John 3:16 NLT). The wages of sin is eternal death, but the gift of God is eternal life through Christ Jesus, our Lord. For it is by grace you have been saved, through faith, and this not from yourselves; it is a gift of God, not by works, so that no one can boast (Ephesians 2:8–9 NLT). If you confess with your mouth, "Jesus is Lord," and believe in your heart that God raised him from the dead, you will be saved (Romans 10:9 NIV). The Lord is patient for your sake. He does not want anyone to perish, so he is giving more time for everyone to repent (2 Peter 3:9 NLT).

Salvation is a work of the Holy Spirit in a person's life. Believing in Jesus Christ is the only way to be saved, but to all who believed him and accepted him, he gave the right to become children of God (John 1:12 NLT). Jesus said,

"I am the way, the truth, and the life. No one can come to the Father except through me" (John 14:6 NLT). He gives eternal life to each one you have given him. And this is the way to have eternal life: to know you, the only true God, and Jesus Christ, the one you sent to earth (John 17:2–3 NLT). Receiving salvation means we must turn from our sins (Acts 2:37–38 NLT). Receiving salvation is simple and personal (Romans 10:8–10 NLT). For if you confess with your mouth that Jesus is Lord and believe in your heart that God raised him from the dead, you will be saved. For it is by believing in your heart that you are made right with God, and it is by confessing with your mouth that you are saved (Romans 10:9–10 NLT). Salvation rescues you from Satin's dominion; for he has rescued us from the one who rules in the kingdom of darkness (Satan), and he has brought us into the Kingdom of his dear Son (Colossians 1:13–14). God has purchased our freedom with his blood and has forgiven all our sins; our salvation is received by Jesus's blood. He paid for you with the precious life blood of Christ, the sinless, spotless Lamb of God (1 Peter 1:19 NLT).

To receive salvation, all you have to do is offer a prayer of faith to receive it. Get alone to a place where you can pray. You can pray this simple prayer: Father, God, I come to you a sinner. I repent of my sins and ask Jesus Christ to come into my heart and forgive me of my sins and cleanse me from all unrighteousness. I now turn away from my sinful nature and ask Jesus to be the Lord of my life. Amen.

If you prayed this prayer in faith, I believe your spirit is reborn. Pray for God to send you to a Bible-based church where you will be taught the word of God. Praise God that you are now a citizen of heaven. I recommend you get a

Bible to read, study, and apply God's word in your life. I recommend an indexed New Living Translation Bible. It is easy to read and understand. Start by reading the book of John in the New Testament. You can read Proverbs, Genesis, and Psalms. You can begin to read Matthew until Revelation. Read one chapter a day; this will only take a few minutes. Read slowly and ask God to give you revelation of his word. Jesus was baptized; he gave us that example. You should also be baptized.

God's Holy Spirit now resides in your body. He will be your teacher, guide, compass, and convictor of sin in your life. The Holy Spirit will lead you to God's truth, but can be grieved. The Holy Spirit is grieved when you murmur, complain, gossip, disobey, disrespect, or talk coarsely. Ask for God's forgiveness in Jesus's name and go on with your life. Once you confess your sins, God will forgive, forget, and remember them no more. Ask God to fill you with his Holy Spirit so that you can have spiritual power in your life to defeat the evil and advance the kingdom of God.

CHAPTER 4

God the Father, God the Son (Jesus), God the Holy Spirit

All three work in unison in our life. God the Father created the heavens and the earth.

He created the sky, the seas, land, and every sort of seed-bearing plants and trees. He created the fish in the sea and the birds of the air. He created every kind of animal: livestock, small animals, and wildlife. He created all human beings with Adam and Eve (Genesis 1 NLT).

God always was and forever shall be. God knew you before you were formed in your mother's womb. God knows your beginning all the way through to the end of your life. God always knows what you think, so it is no surprise to him whatever you do. God loves you so much; he thinks about you all the time. He even knows the number of hairs on your head. God has plans to prosper you to do well. He has a purpose and a plan for your life. If you seek him, he will reveal it to you. For those who belong to Christ, God causes everything to work together for good, according to his purpose. God speaks to us through his Word, his Holy Spirit, and nature. In fact, the Bible tells us that there is no excuse for humankind not to know him because of his creation.

We have this assurance of God: Those who belong to God will live; their bodies will rise again (Isaiah 26:19 NLT).

The Names of God

The names of God in the Bible reveal his character and his nature. Here are names as listed in the Bible: Advocate, the Resurrection, Most High, God of Gods, King of Glory, the Almighty, the Lord of Hosts, Great and Awesome God, My Strength, Everlasting God, Eternal God, Ancient of Days, Living God, Creator of Heaven and Earth, Consuming Fire, Holy Lawgiver, Righteous Father, Righteous Judge, the Lord Who Sanctifies You, Wonderful, Immortal, Invisible, Sovereign God, High Tower, Helper, My Glory, My Strength, Refuge, Shelter, Strong Fortress, Stronghold of My Life, Healer, Hope, Light Spring of Living Water, Sustainer of My Soul, Compassion, God and Father of Our Lord Jesus Christ, Jealous and Avenging God, Gracious God, Faithful God, God of Truth, Forgiving God, God of All Comfort, God of Love and Peace, Encourager, Merciful God, True God, Deliverer, God Our Savior, and Redeemer.

God the Son, Jesus

God sent his Son into the world as a sacrifice for our sins and to redeem us back to God. The Bible tells us that all have sinned and fall short of God's glory. There is no other name that can bring salvation but Jesus.

Jesus tells us in the gospels that we can have anything we need, according to God's will, if we pray in his name. Jesus has given us authority over the devil. We should use his name to defeat the enemy and take back what he stole.

Satan came to kill, steal, and destroy, but Jesus came so that we can enjoy life and live in the abundance of his grace and mercy. Don't let the devil steal your joy, kill your dreams, or destroy your life. You can defeat the devil with the name of Jesus, the blood of Jesus, and the word of God.

In Christ, you will have power, peace, love, joy, and hope. We have the victory in Jesus Christ. In him, we live and move and have our being (Acts 17:28 NKJV).

As a Christian, you became a joint heir with Jesus. Whatever Jesus has, you can have, if you believe and have faith. Since we are God's children, we will share his treasures, for everything God gives to his Son, Christ, is ours too. But if we are to share his glory, we must also share his suffering (Romans 8:16–17 NLT).

The Names of Jesus

The names of Jesus reveal his character and his nature. Here are names of Jesus listed in the Bible: Advocate, Lamb of God, the Resurrection and the Life, Shepherd, Bishop of

Souls, Judge, Lord of Lords, Man of Sorrows, Head of the Church, Master, Faithful and True Witness, Rock, High Priest, the Door, Living Water, Bread of Life, Rose of Sharon, Alpha and Omega, True Vine, Messiah, Teacher, Holy One, Mediator, the Beloved, Branch, Carpenter, Good Shepherd, Light of the World, Image of the Invisible God, the Word, Chief Cornerstone, Savior, Servant. Author and Finisher of Our Faith, the Almighty, Lion of the Tribe of Judah, King of Kings, Prince of Peace, Bridegroom, Only Begotten Son, Wonderful Counselor, Immanuel, Son of Man, Day Spring, Prophet, Redeemer, Anchor, Bright Morning Star, the Way, the Truth, and the Life.

God the Holy Spirit

The Holy Spirit lives in us when we receive salvation. The Holy Spirit will guide us in God's truth. He will lead us, teach us, and warn us of danger. The Holy Spirit is a person who has feelings. We can bring sorrow to the Holy Spirit by the way we live: bitterness, rage, anger, harsh words, gossip, slander, and all types of malicious behavior (Ephesians 4:31 NLT).

The Holy Spirit gives us power to witness about Jesus (Acts1:8 NLT). The Holy Spirit reveals the deep secrets of God (1 Corinthians 2:10 NLT). The Holy Spirit can pray through us. Sometimes, we do not know what to pray for our circumstances or for others, but the Holy Spirit knows. The Bible tells us to pray with understanding and in the Spirit. The Holy Spirit gives us utterance that we do not know, but God knows. Ask God to fill you with the Holy Spirit so that you can pray in the Spirit.

The Holy Spirit is the Spirit of truth. The world cannot accept him; it neither sees him nor knows him (John 14:17 NLT).

The fruit of the Holy Spirit is love, joy, peace, patience, kindness, goodness, and faithfulness (Galatians 5:22–23 NLT).

The Holy Spirit is the Spirit of wisdom and understanding, the Spirit of counsel and might, the Spirit of knowledge, and the fear of the Lord (Isaiah 11:2 NLT).

These are the nine gifts of the Holy Spirit: word of wisdom, word of knowledge, gift of faith, gift of healing, working of miracles, prophesy, discerning of spirits, different kind of tongues (prayer language), and interpretation of tongues (1 Corinthians 12:8–9 NLT).

It is the one and only Holy Spirit who distributes these gifts. He alone decides which gift each person should have. These gifts are to be used to build up the body of Christ (Christians). Ask the Holy Spirit to reveal which gift you are to have.

The Holy Spirit is our comforter and gives us peace. The Holy Spirit desires to be a part of your everyday life. He can warn you when you are about to make a wrong decision or when you are in danger. You will feel a check in your spirit, a feeling of uneasiness. He will give you peace as he leads and guides you. Ask the Holy Spirit to help you make decisions and solve problems. The Holy Spirit is a person, so we should talk to him daily. Tell him how much you appreciate him in your life.

Spend time alone with God, turn off the noise, and wait patiently to hear what the Holy Spirit is saying to you.

You can be filled with the Holy Spirit, by the preaching of the Good News of the gospel of Jesus Christ. In Acts chapter 10, Peter was preaching about Jesus when all who heard the message received the Holy Spirit. They began to speak in tongues (Holy Spirit language) and praising God.

You can be filled with the Holy Spirit by the laying on of hands. When Paul placed his hands on the apostles, the Holy Spirit came on them, and they spoke in other tongues and prophesied (Acts 19:6 NLT). And the Father who knows all hearts knows what the Spirit is saying, for the Spirit pleads for us believers in harmony with God's own will (Romans 8:27 NLT). God has given us his Spirit so we can know the wonderful things he has freely given us (1 Corinthians 2:12 NLT).

The names of the Holy Spirit reveal his character and nature. Names of the Holy Spirit in the Bible are Author of Scripture, Comforter, Counselor, Advocate, Convictor of Sin, Seal, Guide, Indweller of Believers, Intercessor, Revealer, Spirit of Truth, Spirit of God, Spirit of Life, Teacher, and Witness.

CHAPTER 5

Faith

F aith moves God into action. What is faith? It is the confident assurance that what we hope for is going to happen. It is evidence of things we cannot yet see (Hebrews 11:1 NLT). If you can see it, then it is not faith. The Bible says without faith, it is impossible to please God.

Faith without doubt is required in our prayers for God to answer them. Faith comes from listening to the message of the Good News: the Good News about Jesus Christ (Romans 10:17 NLT). The only thing that counts is faith expressing itself through love (Galatians 5:6 NIV). So you see, it isn't enough just to have faith. Faith that doesn't show itself by good deeds is no faith at all; it is dead and useless (James 2:17 NLT).

Faith is a defensive weapon. Faith can extinguish all the flaming arrows (attacks) of the evil one (Hebrews 10:22 NLT).

Since we have been justified through faith, we can have

peace with God through our Lord Jesus Christ (Romans 5:1 NIV).

Your faith can heal you (Matthew 9:29 NIV). We see in the Bible that Jesus told those who had faith they would be healed. We see examples with the woman who had issues with blood, the centurion soldier who had a sick slave, and the Samaritan woman who pleaded with Jesus for her demon-possessed daughter. Jesus told all of them they were healed because of their faith. Trials and tribulations will help you grow in faith and show you how much you depend on God. Your faith will be rewarded here on earth, as well as in heaven.

CHAPTER 6

Temptation: You Can Overcome It

Satan is the tempter. Satan tempted Eve to eat the forbidden fruit from the tree God commanded Adam and Eve not to eat. It was pleasing to her sight, so she ate it and gave some to her husband, Adam, and sin entered the world.

Temptations that come into your life are no different from what others experience. God is faithful. He will keep the temptation from becoming so strong that you can't stand up against it (1 Corinthians 10:13 NLT).

We are to run away from temptation. The best way to avoid temptations is to run from anything that stimulates lust.

Jesus understands our weakness, for he faced all of the same temptations we do, yet he did not sin. So come boldly to the throne of God's grace to help you when you need it (Hebrews 4:16 NLT). Because Jesus suffered when he was tempted, he is able to help those who are being tempted (Hebrews 2:18 NLT).

If sinners entice you, do not give in to them (Proverbs 1:10 NIV). Do not offer the parts of your body to sin, as instruments of wickedness, but rather offer yourself to God (Romans 6:13 NIV).

Temptation usually comes as a pleasant but evil desire of our flesh. Its enjoyment leads to sin. When sin is fulfilled then remorse follows. We are stuck with a guilty conscience and the consequences of our choice. We must repent immediately and ask for God's forgiveness so we can be reconciled with him and be relieved from a guilty conscious. Although our sins are forgiven, we will still have to live with the consequences. We must also forgive ourselves to be free from condemnation.

King David lusted after Uriah's wife, Bathsheba; he committed adultery, and she became pregnant. He summoned Uriah from the battlefield so he could sleep with his wife. Uriah refused to go home because he felt it was not right for him to enjoy the pleasure of his wife while Israel was in battle. King David gave Uriah a sealed letter to give to his commander, which was his death sentence. It placed him in the front line, the fiercest of battle, and he was killed. David committed not only adultery but also murder. Since Bathsheba was pregnant, David decided to marry her. God told David because of his sins, the child would die. God also told David that strife and the sword would never leave his household.

Sin is fun for a season, but there is a price to pay, for the wages of sin is death. If sin was not pleasurable, people would not do it. When evil thoughts come your way, repel them and think about something else. The Bible tells us to take every evil thought captive. We must tackle it with the Word of God.

Temptation runs rampart in our society today. We have sex, drugs, and alcohol to escape from our troubles. There is the internet and social media, where your mind can wander off into the land of temptation. The desire for money and fame can be a tempter to your life. Temptation is a distraction from God's purpose for your life. The devil is the tempter, so when you are tempted, you are to resist the devil, submit it to God, and then the devil will flee. Sexual immorality (natural or unnatural) has caused many sexually transmitted diseases, which can be fatal. The sure cure is abstinence before marriage.

Temptation is usually subtle, like a puppy dog wanting to be petted. In actuality, it is the devil roaming around, seeking someone he can devour. Temptation comes from the lure of our evil desires. These evil desires lend to evil actions, and evil actions lead to death (James 1:14–15 NLT). Pray that you will not be overcome by temptation (Luke 22:40 NLT). We are tempted when we seek pleasure rather than God. God allows temptation in our life. He gives us a free will to choose evil or good.

No temptation has seized you except what is common to man. And God is faithful; he will not let you be tempted beyond what you can bear. But when you are tempted, he will also provide a way out so that you can stand up under it (1 Corinthians 10:13 NIV).

By reading, studying, and applying the Word of God to your life, you can overcome temptation. Fill your mind with good thoughts; when you do this, there is not room for evil thoughts. If evil thoughts come in, speak out with a positive one.

Sin is an entrapment by Satan with a death sentence. Tell Satan he is the father of lies and there is no truth in him. Say, "Satan, your future is in the fiery furnace of hell. My future is in heaven."

Satan, the blood of Jesus comes against you. No weapon formed against you will prosper. You can do all things through Christ. Satan, you do not have authority over me. I resist you in the name of Jesus, and you must flee. Speak the Word of God with boldness to defeat the enemy. Ask God to help you overcome your temptation.

Temptation comes from your own lustful desires: lust of the flesh, lust of the eyes, and the pride of life. The devil knows your weakest point and will attack when you are most vulnerable.

Stay away from the things that tempt you. If you lust after the bodies of others, then bounce your eyes so as to not focus on them. Remember: They are made in the image of God. That should deter you.

If you lust after things that others have, it will turn into jealousy. Instead, think about what you do have, and thank God for them. If you are full of pride and boast about all you have and what you have done, God will resist you. Instead, humble yourself before almighty God and walk in humility. Recognize that God gave you the ability to work and gain wealth.

If you have wealth, don't be tempted to buy everything your heart desires. Think about the poor, the hungry, the widows, and the orphans. Invest in them, and then you will have treasures in heaven.

CHAPTER 7

Know Your Enemy

S atan is the spirit of antichrist. The spirit of antichrist is blinding the minds of those who do not believe in Jesus Christ and his power. They seek the pleasures of life instead of God. It is moving in our society like I have never seen before. Rioters seeking to disrupt political meetings with destruction of property; they are doing the devil's work. It seems like the thought police (political correctness) has intruded every institution of our society.

In February 2017, Senator David Cassidy held a town hall meeting in Breaux Bridge, Louisiana. There were a bunch of cars with out-of-state license plates. This was a coordinated, organized protest to disrupt the meeting. Before the meeting started, a chaplain began with a prayer. Shouts of, "Go pray on your own time," were chanted.

When the chaplain was closing the prayer saying, "In Jesus's name," there was jeers of hissing. The conservative people of Louisiana would never disrespect the name of Jesus. Things got out of hand, with loud booing and sneering that kept Senator Cassidy from his agenda. The rioters were successful in their mission of disrupting the town hall meeting.

The spirit of antichrist is trying to impede our nation internally. Again, evildoers are seeking to codify into law their immorality. We already have abortion and same-sex marriage. Political correctness is a movement that threatens our Christian values and freedoms.

Chaplains in our military are told not to pray in Jesus's name or they will be disciplined. Soldiers are told not to share their faith or they will be demoted, discharged, or transferred.

Christian bakers are fined because of their refusal to participate in homosexual marriages.

The presidential election was a spiritual battle for the soul of our nation. Antichrist people are outraged that their candidate lost the election. They are in rebellion, not wanting to lose their evil ground. They see President Trump and conservatives as a threat to their immoral behavior and will do anything possible to stop the president and his agenda.

Antichrist people in society have pressured government officials into removing the Ten Commandments from our institutions. They are rewriting history to remove God and Jesus Christ from our school textbooks. These rebellious people want no restraints on their immoral behavior.

Satan blinds the eyes and minds of those who are ignorant of the gospel of Jesus Christ.

With the election of Donald Trump as president, we have been given an open door to take back the ground we have lost over the past decades and turn our nation back to

God. Let us not shrink back. Failure is not an option for Christians. Godliness exalts a nation, but sin is a disgrace to any people (Proverbs 14:34 NLT).

There is even an antichrist organization called Freedom from Religion Foundation, which is the hub for agnostics and atheists. The spokesman for this organization claims to be a lifelong atheist and is not afraid to burn in hell.

How far has our nation gone from its origin of freedom of religion and one nation under God? Where is our nation heading? The only way for America to turn back to God: if Christians pray fervently for God to turn our nation back to him. In our beginning as a nation, Congress approved and financed the first textbook in public school: the Bible. Judges wore white gloves and were required to be Christians so that justice would be given with sound biblical judgment.

We are in a pleasure-seeking generation, which is the enemy of God's purpose for us.

CHAPTER 8

～✦～

We Are in a Spiritual War

B e careful. Watch out for attacks from the devil, your great enemy. He prowls around like a roaring lion, looking for some victim to devour (1 Peter 5:8 NLT). The devil's job is to kill, steal, and destroy. Satan wants to kill your destiny with God, steal your joy, and destroy your life. Jesus came that we can enjoy life and live more abundantly.

Satan wages an all-out battle for your soul. He will try in various ways to stop you from knowing and believing in Jesus Christ. He uses pride, a sense that you don't need God to accomplish what you want in life. He wants you to walk in ignorance of the Gospel of Jesus Christ so he can steal your soul. He wants to use you to do his will, not God's. Satan uses all kinds of addictions, strongholds, and mind-sets to keep you bound. Jesus Christ gives us freedom from bondage and gives us liberty to live free from the enemy's stronghold and for the glory of God.

God gives us armor for the battles we face against Satan.

The apostle Paul gives us an analogy of the Roman soldier's armor to go into battle:

The Helmet of Salvation

Lord, protect my mind and thoughts from the attacks of the enemy. Help me, Lord, to think like a Christian. I take every thought captive to the obedience of Christ. The battle with the enemy is won or lost in your mind. Thank the Lord for your salvation.

The Breastplate of Righteousness

Our righteousness comes from Jesus Christ. We are made right with God through the blood of Jesus. The breastplate covers the heart. Lord, protect my heart from the enemy's attack. Keep your heart open to God and closed to sin. Put on faith and love as your breastplate. We have righteousness as our weapons, both to attack and to defend.

The Strong Belt of Truth

Lord, sturdy my faith with your truth. Help me live in the truth and speak the truth in love. Lord, give me discernment from the lies of the devil.

The Gospel Shoes of Peace

Fill me with your peace, Lord Jesus. I pray that your peace will guide me.

The Shield of Faith

Lord, protect me from the fiery darts of the enemy. Without faith, it is impossible to please God. Pray that your faith will not fail.

The Sword of the Spirit, which is the Word of God

Take the Word of God and wield it against the enemy. Speak the Word of God in faith to defeat the enemy and advance the Kingdom of God (Ephesians 6:13–17 NLT).

Pray God's Word over your circumstance; God's Word is his will for your life. Fight the enemy with the name of Jesus, the blood of Jesus, and the Word of God. For though we live in the world, we do not wage spiritual warfare as the world does: The weapons we fight with are not the weapons of the world; on the contrary, they have divine power to demolish the devil's strongholds. We demolish arguments and every pretention that sets itself against the knowledge of God, and we take captive every thought to make it obedient to Christ (2 Corinthians 10:3–5 NIV).

Satan wants the soul of individuals as well as our nation. Failure is not an option; we must battle the enemy with spiritual warfare. We must pray with understanding and in the Spirit. We must fast to increase our spiritual power. We must speak the Word of God in faith; no weapons formed against you will prosper. We must pray for ourselves as well as our leaders so that we may live in peace. We have victory in Christ Jesus. We do not wrestle against flesh and blood but against principalities, against powers, against the rulers of the darkness of this age, against spiritual hosts of wickedness in the heavenly places (Ephesians 6:12 KJV).

CHAPTER 9

God's Forgiveness Is for You

When you give your life to Jesus and ask for the forgiveness of your sins, God will forgive you of your sins and remember them no more. Sometimes, you may still feel guilty, even though you confessed your sin. You must forgive yourself so you can be free of condemnation. The scriptures tell you that you are free from condemnation; you must act accordingly.

The Bible tells us, "If we confess our sins, God is faithful and just to forgive us of our sins and cleanse us from all unrighteousness" (1 John 1:9 KJV).

God commands you to forgive others. If you don't forgive others of their sin against you, then your sins will not be forgiven (Matthew 6:15 NIV). When you don't forgive, God allows tormenting spirits to wreak havoc in your life.

One of the biggest hindrances to a Christian's walk with Jesus is not forgiving. In my own experiences in life, I was easily offended and would often avoid that person for what they had done to me. I chose to be angry with them. Later, I realized that anger was a form of pride. Think about it: The main reason you get angry is because you did not get your way. As I read the scriptures on unforgiveness, conviction came over me. I was actually hurting myself instead of punishing the other person. The scriptures tell us that our prayers will not be answered because of unforgiveness. I had to repent and forgive that person as long as it took until I had victory in that area. Now, forgiveness is easy for me because I was able to conquer unforgiveness. God puts trials in your way so your faith can grow.

God has rescued us from the one who rules in the kingdom of darkness, and he has brought us into the kingdom of his dear Son. God has purchased our freedom with his blood and has forgiven all our sins (Colossians 1:13 NLT).

I remember this young man I ministered to on forgiveness and the consequences of not forgiving. He was shy and introverted. His countenance was down, and he did not have much hope about his future. He told me his boss had fired him and that he was angry at him for doing so. After he received the revelation of forgiveness, he drove from Baton Rouge to Houston. The very next day, he met with his former boss and confessed his bitterness and anger, and then he told him that he had forgiven him and asked for his former boss to forgive him. The two were reconciled, and he drove back a changed man. I noticed how happy he had become. He was full of excitement about Jesus and full of hope for his future.

On another occasion, I was teaching this principle in the Salvation Army transit unit. There was a young man there who did not want to hear what I had to say, but the Holy

Spirit quickened him to get out of his bed and listen to the message. After sharing my testimony and sharing the good news about forgiveness and reconciliation, he came forward to receive prayer. He hated his mother for something done in the past and had not been in contact with her for some time. He was able to forgive, then his heart softened, and he was able to reconcile with his mother.

God has given us the gift of reconciliation so that we can use our experience that we went through to minister to others. Don't be discouraged when you go through a trial. God can use you to help others.

CHAPTER 10

God Answers Prayer

P rayer is simply talking to God, telling him of your needs and thanking him for what he will do for you. Also thank God for all that he has done for you.

In God's world, you must have faith and believe that he will answer your prayer. You need to believe before you receive. Wait on God; focus on him and his promises. If you are in sin, ask God to forgive you in Jesus's name. God will answer your prayer in one of three ways: yes, wait, or no.

Know that all things work together for good for those who love the Lord and are called according to his purpose (Romans 8:28 KJV).

God is love, God is full of mercy, and God is full of grace. You may not know or understand why things are happening to you or a loved one, but God knows. You may never find out why someone has fallen sick or died, but he knows.

Some answers you won't know until you get to heaven.

God wants you to live by faith and obedience, and he will take care of the rest.

God is a rewarder of those who diligently seek him. Tell God, Jesus, and the Holy Spirit that you love them. They all have feelings, and they can be happy or sad at what we do.

I begin each day by telling God, "I love you." I tell Jesus, "I love you." I tell the Holy Spirit, "I love you." I tell the Holy Spirit he is welcome in my place. Ask God what he wants you to do. If you are in tune with the Holy Spirit, you will get an impression of what God wants you to do.

God will give you peace when you offer your prayer in faith, knowing that he will answer it. It is a feeling that no matter the outcome, you will be okay with that. Remember that your joy in the Lord is your strength. You can sense God's presence as he is directing your path. The Lord delights in the prayer of the upright (Proverbs 15:8 NLT). He hears the prayers of the righteous (Proverbs 15:29 NLT).

God can give you an idea to open a business, write a book, or start a ministry. He can help you solve difficult problems.

I heard about a woman who graduated from college and incurred a huge student loan debt of $40,000. She was now working but could not conceive of anyway to pay it back. She prayed for God's help. She prayed often for God to answer her prayer. One day, someone from the university called and told her they decided to forgive all of her debt. Isn't God good?

I went to India a few years ago on a mission trip. We were paired in two or three then sent out into villages with a minister. Most people spoke English, but some did not. I remember this woman minister named Cinderella; I called her God's princess because she was truly a servant of the most high God. She asked us to pray for a godly woman who had a malignant tumor in her abdomen about the size of a baseball.

We laid hands on her and began to pray. As we were praying, the tumor began to dissolve until there was nothing left of it. We were so thankful that God had answered our prayer.

Another amazing thing I witnessed was that people could sense the presence of God on us and invited us to come pray a blessing over their home.

Jesus sent his disciples in pairs to go out to the village and do the works of the Lord: cast out demons and heal the sick, the blind, and the deaf. They were to stay in one home and give it their blessing. If the family deserved, the blessing stayed, but if they were undeserving, the blessing would return to the disciples.

Jesus tells us, "Where two or three are gathered in my name, there I am in the midst of them" (Matthew 18:20 KJV).

You may cry out to God in desperation or a simple request. He hears your prayer and is moved by faith. The Bible tells us that without faith, it is impossible to please him. So now we know that he absolutely loves faith and is willing to move heaven and earth for those who walk by faith.

Jesus said, "If you have faith the size of a mustard seed, you can tell this mountain to be thrown into the sea and it will happen" (Matthew 17:20 NKJV). What Jesus was saying is that it only takes a little faith for God to give you the victory in your circumstance. Your heavenly Father will give good gifts to those who ask him (Matthew 7:11 NLT). If you believe, you will receive whatever you ask for in prayer (Matthew 21:2 NLT).

Delight yourself also in the Lord, and he will give you the desires and secret petitions of your heart (Psalm 31:4 NIV).

Always be joyful. Keep on praying, no matter what happens; always be thankful, for this is the Lord's will for you who belong to Christ Jesus (1 Thessalonians 5:16–18 NLT).

CHAPTER 11

Hope

"Hope" is defined in *Webster's Dictionary* as a desire with expectation of fulfillment. So what desire are we pursuing? There is only one true hope that is worth pursuing because it has eternal value, which is Jesus Christ. In this life, our human desires are short-lived. The truth is, you will never be satisfied with human desire. God did not make us that way. Our desires are misplaced when we try to keep up with our neighbors or when we desire a bigger house than is needed, expensive cars, clothing, jewelry, and other indulgences.

Hope comes from faith. We have faith in God that what we hope for, he will bring to pass. I am not talking about just anything but God's will for your life. Some things are beneficial in what we hope for but have no eternal value.

In the Old Testament, God reminded the Israelites through the prophets to put their hope in the Lord, for the Lord offers unfailing love and full redemption. He will redeem Israel from all their sins (Psalm 30:7–8 NIV).

But time after time, the nation of Israel would turn away from God and place their hope in false gods and idols. Then God would raise up their enemy to defeat them. When Israel would cry out to God, he would relent and set them free. You would think they'd learn their lesson from past mistakes. One generation would put their hope in God, then the next generation, who had not experienced what God had done, would turn away from him.

God is the same yesterday, today, and forever. God will not let sin go unpunished. This truth still applies today in America. Going back to the birth of our nation, people came from Europe to escape religious tyranny so they could be free to worship. Our forefathers established a religious heritage, which has been kept from generation to generation. Is it a wonder why America has been so blessed and great for so many years? God's hand of protection has been on us for so long that we take it for granted.

Our nation has slowly but methodically turned its back on God. God warned us not to take this slippery slope or face consequences. He allowed terrorist attacks on our nation. Our biggest attack that comes to mind was September 11, 2001. God took his hand of protection off our nation that day, and we saw the results. The twin towers in New York were demolished, killing and injuring thousands. Americans lost billions of dollars overnight in the stock market. The Pentagon was hit to give us warning about the decline of our military power. The third airplane to go down crashed in an open field. It was intended to hit the US Capitol to disrupt our government and create chaos in our nation. God was sending us a message that our wealth, protection, and power as a nation would be in jeopardy if we did not put our hope in him. The Sunday after 9/11 was the highest church attendance in history. Many Christians have connected the dots that led to 9/11 and are still committed to pray for America. But the vast majority of Americans are clueless as to why this happened. Our nation has become desensitized to the reality of God, his sovereignty, and his judgment. If we as a nation refuse to put our hope in God, he will send more terrorists into our country to wreak havoc, confusion, destruction, and panic. We will have peace as long as we put our hope in God.

God made us so that we would put our hope in him. He will be our provider, our source, our health, our freedom, our protection, our confidence, our peace, and our trust in him. Jesus is the hope of the entire world (Matthew 12:21 NLT).

CHAPTER 12

Joy

Webster's Dictionary defines "joy" as an emotion evoked by well-being, success, or good fortune; characterized by gladness or delight.

God wants us to have joy in our life. He has given us the tools to use to insure joy in our life by his promises in the Bible. Joy is a pleasant feeling that you are blessed by God. It is a restful assurance that God has your backside and will help you go through the difficulties in life. Your joy is complete in the Lord Jesus Christ. The devil will try to steal your joy if you let him. Psalm 16:11 (NIV) says, "You have made known to me the path of life; you will fill me with joy in your presence, with eternal pleasures at your right hand." The world can offer you joy for a season, but God's joy in you will be for eternity. Jesus said, "Ask and you will receive and your joy will be complete" (John 16:24 NIV).

Jesus tells us to seek first the kingdom of God and his righteousness and things we hope for will be given to us.

For the Kingdom of God is righteousness, peace, and joy in the Holy Spirit.

When the Holy Spirit controls your life, he will produce this kind of fruit: love, joy, peace, patience, kindness, goodness, faithfulness, gentleness, and self-control (Galatians 5:22 NLT).

If you want the Holy Spirit to control your life, you must submit to Jesus as your Lord and Savior. Submission is the key for joy in your life. Those who belong to Christ Jesus have nailed the passions and desires of their sinful nature to his cross and crucified them there (Galatians 5:24 NLT). Happy are those who fear the Lord. Yes, happy are those who delight in doing what he commands (Psalm 112:1 NLT)

Happy is the person who finds wisdom and gains understanding (Proverbs 3:13 NLT).

CHAPTER 13

Laughter

The Bible says that laughter is a good medicine. Let's look at the benefits of laughter:

- lowers your blood pressure
- reduces your stress hormone levels
- works your abs
- improves your cardiac health
- produces a general sense of well-being
- boosts your immune system
- builds your confidence
- enhances your intake of oxygen-rich air
- stimulates your heart, lungs, and muscles
- helps to reduce pain
- reduces depression
- boosts your relationships
- improves your breathing
- helps you lose weight
- helps you feel accepted

What we need more of as Christians is laughter. People are drawn to humor. It makes them feel comfortable around us when we laugh. I heard a story of a well-known comedian who had a promising future. A major television network offered him a million dollars a week to be in a sitcom. He decided to use his humor to advance the Kingdom of God. He has had more than twenty-eight thousand people receive Christ in his ministry. He has a great gift and is using it to glorify God. How much more can we glorify God and advance the Kingdom of God when we use humor?

The average child laughs four hundred times a day, while an adult laughs only four times a day. Jesus said that we must have faith like a little child to enter the Kingdom of heaven. If we laugh like a little child, then we will have a happier and healthier life. If you have difficulty with laughter, then watch funny movies, read joke books, or hang around people who have the gift of humor.

CHAPTER 14

Holy Living

God said, "You must be holy because I am holy" (1 Peter 1:16 NLT). What does that mean? My first reaction to this scripture is that you must be perfect in all you are and what you do. This is an impossible standard for anyone except Jesus, but this is not what God means. "Holy" means being set apart. You are to be set apart from the filth of sin in this world that would corrupt you. That does not mean you can never sin. It is by God's grace that your sins are forgiven; Jesus paid that price. You are not given a license to sin but the grace to overcome its power over you.

You are set apart to do the will of God, advancing the Kingdom of God. In view of God's mercy, you are to offer your body as a living sacrifice, holy and pleasing to God; this is your true and proper worship (Romans 12:1 NIV).

CHAPTER 15

Keep Your Heart Soft

In the Bible, the heart is referred to as the soul and spirit. When we get saved, our spirit and soul are reborn; it is soft and pliable. In Matthew chapter 13 (NLT), Jesus describes four different conditions of the heart:

As the farmer scatters seed across his field, some fell on the footpath, and birds came and ate them. The seed represents the Word of God. The seeds fell on the hard footpath, which represents a hard heart. A hard heart cannot receive the Word of God because the devil comes in and snatches it away, so there is no harvest.

Some seeds fell on shallow soil with underlying rock. At first, the seeds sprout and begin to grow, but their roots are too shallow. This represents those who receive the Word of God with joy and at first get along fine, but they wilt as soon as they have problems or are persecuted because they believe the Word.

Some seeds fell on thorny ground, which represents those who hear and accept the Good News. But all too quickly, the message is crowded out by the cares of this life and the lure of wealth, so no crop is produced.

Some seeds fell on good soil, which represents the hearts of those who truly accept God's message and produce a huge harvest: thirty, sixty, or even one hundred times as much as had been planted (Matthew 13:1–23 NLT).

The Bible tells us to guard our heart, for the issues of life will come against it. Let faith and love cover your heart. Walk in humility, trust God, read the Word, and spend time with God, Jesus, and the Holy Spirit.

If you do these things, you will keep your heart soft, and it will produce a huge harvest.

CHAPTER 16

Grace and Mercy

"Grace" means to get something you do not deserve. "Mercy" means you do not get the punishment that you deserve.

John 1:15–17 (NIV) says, "For the law was given through Moses: grace and truth came through Jesus Christ." For it is by grace you have been saved, through faith, and this not from yourselves; it is the gift of God (Ephesian 2:8 NIV).

Let us then approach the throne of grace with confidence, so that we will receive mercy and find grace to help us in our time of need (Hebrews 4:16 NIV).

See to it that no one fails to obtain the grace of God; that no "root of bitterness" springs up and causes trouble and by it many become defiled (Hebrews 12:15 NIV).

After you have suffered a little while, the God of all grace, who has called you to his eternal glory in Christ, will himself restore, confirm, strengthen, and establish you (1 Peter 5:10 NIV).

God opposes the proud but gives grace to the humble (James 4:6 NIV).

God's punishment for sin has always been to bring sinners to repentance so they can be restored back to God.

God is full of grace and mercy. I am living proof of that. He could have let me die on three separate occasions, but his grace and mercy intervened.

It is hard to comprehend the concept of grace and mercy, but as Christians, we trust God and take him at his word. Let us then approach the throne of grace with confidence, so that we will receive mercy and find grace to help us in our time of need (Hebrews 4:16 NIV).

Our salvation comes by God's grace. For it is by grace you have been saved, through faith, and this not from yourselves; it is the gift of God (Ephesians 2:8 NIV).

The law was given by Moses, which convicts us of our sin. Grace and truth came through Jesus Christ so that our sins may be forgiven. But God is so rich in mercy, and he loved us so very much, that even while we were dead because of our sins, he gave us life when he raised Christ from the dead (Ephesians 2:4 NLT).

Grace is given to the humble. God opposes the proud but gives grace to the humble (James 4:6 NLT).

If you have suffered because of your sin or simply by circumstances, God will restore you when you repent of your sin. After you have suffered a little while, the God of all grace, who has called you to his eternal glory in Christ, will himself restore, confirm, strengthen, and establish you (Peter 5:10 NLT).

Without God's mercy, you will stand before God and

account for the sins in your life. God's judgment will be eternal separation from him. You will spend eternity in hell.

To receive God's mercy, you must become a Christian. Then you will live in eternity in heaven with God. God's mercy is upon generation after generation toward those who fear him (Luke 1:50 NIV).

God has great mercy for Christians. Blessed be the God and Father of our Lord Jesus Christ, who according to his great mercy has caused us to be born again to the living hope through the resurrection of Jesus Christ from the dead (1 Peter 1:3 NLT).

God will show grace and mercy to whomever he desires and will harden the hearts of anyone he chooses. But He has obligated himself to show grace and mercy to his children. If you are not a child of God, simply repent from your sins and ask Jesus to come into your life and forgive you of your sins.

CHAPTER 17

No More Shame

"Shame," defined in *Webster's Dictionary*, is a painful sense of having done something wrong, improper, or immodest; a condition of humiliating, or disrepute.

As you can see, shame is very painful and can haunt you all your life. We all have a shameful past of something we did (or did not do). The devil reminds us of our faults and disgrace. God did not make us to live a disgraceful life. If you confess your sin, God will forgive you and will remember it no more. The problem is we have a hard time forgiving ourselves.

I have struggled with shame most of my life. I grew up shy and introverted. I felt that I did not have anything to say in a conversation. I enjoyed listening to others, but my mind would go blank as to what to say, so I said nothing. I thought of myself as being abnormal, not being able to carry out a conversation. My conversation was usually one or two words or maybe a sentence or two. I felt shameful of things I did wrong. I went through three failed marriages. At times,

I felt that I had no value or worth. I often thought that if I were different, I would be happier. I wanted to be like other people, carrying on conversations and laughing. I am a person who dreams often, almost every night. More often than not, I would dream about my inferiority and things I did wrong. The enemy was playing this over and over in my dreams. I would wake up the next morning and think about what I dreamed and what it meant. I often felt that I would not amount to anything. I was just going through the motions of life. I didn't have any real goals or visions for my future. I felt like a big fat failure. People didn't have to express disappointment or blame me; I did it to myself.

I would put on a happy face, but inside I was unhappy with myself. I often thought, *Why did God create me this way?*

At times, I thought of suicide as a way out. God had other plans for my life. Jesus said, "I came to give you life and abundant living" (John 10:10 KJV). What did he mean by this?

One day, I was listening to Joel Osteen's message on *Shame No More*. The message gave me a new revelation about shame. The Holy Spirit convicts us of sin in our life. God never intended you to live in guilt and condemnation. When you confess your sin, he forgives immediately, and you are free from guilt and condemnation. Our job is to roll back the shame, guilt, and condemnation. You must affirm, "No more shame." Say it aloud: "No more shame." You may have to say this often, day after day, before you get a release.

God always has a redemptive plan for you when you sin. Jesus died on the cross to take away your shame. Stay obedient to God, resist the devil, and he will flee. I find it comforting to tell the devil where he will spend eternity:

in hell. He will be tormented forever with shame, disgrace, and condemnation.

As a Christian, your future is in heaven with God. It is a place free from sin, pain, shame, and condemnation. It is the glorious eternal life God planned for us before we were born.

Our worth comes from God, not people or things we have acquired. You are very valuable and precious to God. He made a way for you to spend eternity in heaven. Jesus payed for our entrance by his shedding his blood on the cross.

CHAPTER 18

Overcoming Worry

W*ebster's Dictionary* defines "worry" as mental distress or agitation resulting from concern for something impending or anticipated; anxiety, nervousness, and uneasiness.

Worry is like sitting in a rocking chair; it keeps you busy, but you are not getting anywhere. Worry is paying interest on anxiety before trouble has even arrived.

The effects of worry can lead to high anxiety and panic. It can affect your appetite, lifestyle, habits, relationships, and sleep. You can't focus on reality or think clearly.

According to WebMD, chronic worry and emotional stress can trigger a host of health problems, including difficulty swallowing, dizziness, dry mouth, fast heartbeat, fatigue, headaches, inability to concentrate, irritability, muscle aches, nausea, nervous energy, rapid breathing, shortness of breath, trembling, and twitching.

It is said that 75 percent of what we worry about will not happen. Most of the things you worry about, you can do nothing about. You can only do something about a small percentage of what you worry about. So the law of averages says that what you worry about will never happen.

Worry is usually a result of fear of the unknown. Fear is the opposite of faith. It means you don't trust God to work on your behalf. The Bible says, "We are to cast our cares unto the Lord" (1 Peter 5:6–7 NIV). We are to humble ourselves before God, casting our cares on him and trusting him. Trust God; that is the only way you can live a worry-free lifestyle. It does not mean you will never fear. We all had some worry or fear in our past. But it doesn't have to define who you are. Faith and the word of God will help you overcome worry. Don't worry about anything; instead, pray about everything. Tell God what you need, and thank him for all he has done (Philippians 4:6 NLT).

Worry will cause you to lose your peace and open a door for the enemy's attack. On the other hand, worship is a weapon against the devil that can bring you peace.

Only you can change your worry habit. You can overcome worry by faith in God and the Word of God. It is also beneficial to read inspirational books on faith, listen to Christian music, and listen to positive preachers like Joel Osteen.

Think of all the good in your life instead of the bad; write it down and refer to it from time to time.

Worry may be hereditary. You may have a personality type that leans on being negative. You will have to work on being positive. Worry can drain you of life itself. You are what you think. Think positive, and more than likely you will get positive results. On the other hand, when you think negatively, you will repel people from you.

Here are some activities that will help with worry: exercise daily, eat a healthy balanced diet, learn to relax, meditate, socialize, and talk to a professional therapist. For chronic worriers, your behavior is a stronghold in your life. It did not happen overnight but occurred over time. You have allowed thoughts to freely come into your mind. You can control your thoughts. The Bible tells us to take every thought captive. The devil will send wrong thoughts your way. You are to take authority over these thoughts and replace them with positive ones.

You are to renew your mind. How do you do this? By reading and studying the Word. This will help transform your mind. Repeat these verses ten times a day: For God has not given me a spirit of fear, but of power, love, and a sound mind (2 Timothy 2:1–7 NLT). For this is the day the Lord has made; let us rejoice and be glad in it (Psalm 118:24 NIV). I choose to be happy today. I expect the best and with God's help will attain the best. There is no fear in love, but perfect love drives out fear (1 John 4:18 NIV). I believe that my mind is now emptied of all anxiety, all fear, and all sense of insecurity. I can do all things with the help of Jesus Christ, who gives me the strength I need (Philippians 4:13 NLT).

Fix your mind with thoughts of faith, confidence, and security. Fix your thoughts on what is true, honorable, and right. Think about things that are pure and lovely and admirable. Think about things that are excellent and worthy of praise (Philippians 4:8 NLT).

When bad thoughts come your way, think about something good. Make no room for wrong thoughts to get into your mind. Above all else, guard your heart, for it affects everything you do (Proverbs 4:2 NLT).

CHAPTER 19

Overcoming Depression

Depression is a condition of sadness, difficulty in thinking and concentration, feelings of dejection, and loss of interest. According to WebMD, the main causes of depression include physical or emotional abuse, death of a loved one, serious illness, substance abuse, lack of hope, and family history of depression.

I suffered from depression for most of my life. I would be happy at times but always returned to depression, without reason. I thought that was normal for me. I got prescriptions for depression medication, but they did not help. I did not have hope for getting better. The Bible says, "Hope deferred makes the heart sad" (Proverbs 13:12 NLT).

Sometimes, depression occurs for a season, and when that season is over, the person bounces back. Other types of depression can last a lifetime. God did not design us to live a depressed life. Faith in God and what Jesus did on the cross can help you overcome depression. It is important to meditate on the promises of God and become what he intended you to be.

If you have depression, see a competent psychiatrist. It may be that you have a chemical imbalance in your brain. A good psychiatrist can give you the correct diagnosis and prescribe the medication for your depression. I was fortunate God sent me to a good psychiatrist, who diagnosed me with a bipolar depression. It took some time, but she was able to find the right medication. I finally realized that I did not have to live with depression.

Things you can do to help with depression:

- get a routine
- set goals
- exercise
- eat healthy
- get enough sleep
- visit a friend
- connect with people on social media
- challenge negative thoughts and change how you think
- do something new: learn to play a musical instrument, work with puzzles, learn a new dance, take up a new hobby, or learn a new language
- try to have fun; make time for things you enjoy, keep going to movies, keep going out with friends for dinner

Remember: Jesus died for you so that you can have abundant living. It's time to claim your healing of depression in Jesus's name. By his bruises, you are healed (Isaiah 53:5 NIV).

CHAPTER 20

The Day of the Lord Is Coming

The Lord's return will happen soon. We do not know the day or the hour, but the signs in the earth are like the birthing pains before the baby comes. We are living in the last days before the Lord's return, so we must be ready, seeking God and doing his will.

The prophet Isaiah from the Old Testament prophesied the future destruction of the earth: "Look! The Lord is about to destroy the earth and make it a vast wasteland. See how he is scattering the people over the face of the earth. The earth will be completely emptied and looted. The Lord has spoken" (Isaiah 24:1–3 NLT).

"The earth dries up, the crops wither, and the skies refuse to rain. The earth suffers from the sins of its people, for they have twisted the instruction of God, violated his laws and broken his everlasting covenant. Therefore, a curse consumes the earth and its people. They are left desolate, destroyed by fire. Few will be left alive. All the joys will be gone. Terror and traps and snares will be your lot, you people of the earth" (Isaiah 24:4–7 NLT).

I must tell you that God's children are citizens of heaven and don't belong to the earth and its destruction.

Isaiah further prophesies, "Destruction falls on you from the heavens. The earth has broken down and has utterly collapsed. Everything is lost, abandoned and confused. The earth staggers like a drunkard. It trembles like a tent in the storm. It falls and will not rise again, for its sins are very great" (Isaiah 24:18–20 NLT).

In that day, the Lord will punish the fallen angels (demons) in the heavens and the proud rulers of the nations on earth. They will be rounded up and put in prison until they are tried and condemned. Then the Lord almighty will mount his throne on Mount Zion. He will rule gloriously in Jerusalem, in the sight of all leaders of his people. There will be such glory that the brightness of the sun and moon will seem to fade away (Isaiah 24:21–23 NLT).

The Hope of Resurrection

In the first book of Thessalonians chapter 4, God reveals to us what will happen to his people when Jesus returns.

For since we believe that Jesus died and was raised to life again, we also believe that when Jesus comes, God will bring back with Jesus all the Christians who have died. We who are still living when the Lord returns will not rise ahead of those who are in their graves; For the Lord, himself, will come down from heaven with a commanding shout, with the call of the archangel, and the trumpet call of God. First all the Christians who have died will rise from their graves. Then, together with them, we who are still alive and remain on the earth will be caught up in the clouds to meet the Lord in the air and remain with him forever. So comfort and encourage each other with these words (1 Thessalonians 4: 14–18 NLT).

The day of the Lord will come unexpectedly, like the thief in the night. When people are saying, "All is well; everything is peaceful and secure," then disaster will fall upon them suddenly as a woman's birth pain begin when her child is about to be born. And there will be no escape (1 Thessalonians 5:2–3 NLT).

The Final Judgment

God will be seated on the great white throne of judgment. The earth and sky fled from his presence, but they found no place to hide. The dead, both great and small, will stand before God's throne, and the books will be opened, including the Book of Life. And the dead will be judged according to the things written in the books, according to what they have done. (Christians will not be judged by God because their names are written in the Book of Life; Jesus will reward us according to our deeds.) And death and the grave were thrown into the lake of fire. This is the second death: the lake of fire. And anyone whose name was not found recorded in the Book of Life was thrown into the lake of fire (Revelation 20:11–15 NLT).

In Matthew 25, Jesus tells of the final judgment. But when the Son of Man, Jesus, comes in his glory, and all the angels with him, then he will sit upon his glorious throne. All the nations will be gathered in his presence, and he will separate them as a shepherd separates the sheep from the goats. The sheep represent the Christians of the world. He will place the sheep at his right hand and the goats on the left. The goats represent those who have rejected Jesus Christ as their Lord and Savior. Then the King will say to those on the right, "Come you who are blessed by my Father, inherit the kingdom prepared for you from the foundation of the world." Then the King will turn to those on the left and say, "Away with you, you cursed ones, into the eternal fire prepared for the Devil and his demons" (Matthew 25:31–4 NLT).

Praise God for your salvation and your eternal reward in heaven.

CHAPTER 21

———— ❧ ————

God's Peace: A Key to Victorious Living

"Peace," defined in *Webster's Dictionary,* is a state of calm and quiet; freedom from disturbing thoughts or emotions; serenity. As you can see, peace is a state of mind we all strive for.

Jesus paid the price for your peace. All you need to do is accept what he did for you on the cross. You must pursue peace because the enemy's desire is for you to worry, complain, criticize others, and lose your peace.

The peace you get from God is far beyond our understanding. Peace from God is everlasting. You can have this peace when you submit to Jesus Christ as your Lord and Savior. Let the peace of Christ rule in your heart and guide you.

God gives you victory through our Lord, Jesus Christ (1 Corinthians 15:57 NLT). It is only through God and Jesus Christ that you will have victory in all areas of your life:

your relationships, your finances, your health, your mind, your emotions, and over the power of sin in your life.

Everyone born of God (spiritual rebirth) overcomes the world; this is the victory that has overcome the world, even our faith. Who is it that overcomes the world? Only he who believes that Jesus is the Son of God (1 John 5:4 NLT).

You are not victorious within yourself, but only through Jesus Christ. In him, you live and move and have your being. Jesus gives you authority to overcome the power of the enemy (Luke 10:19 NLT). If God is for us, who can be against us? (Romans 8:31 NIV).

You are assured in the Holy Scriptures that God is well able to do more abundantly than what you can do or ask for. Jesus came that you may live life more abundantly. That does not mean you won't have difficulties. The Bible promises you will have trials and tribulations, but in Jesus Christ, you can have joy even when going through the worst of times. Your joy is complete in Christ; rest assured that he will help you in your time of need.

There is no affliction, addiction, bad habits, wrong choices, or sin in your life that Jesus can't correct. You must put your trust and hope in God and Jesus Christ. Your past does not define your future. The apostle Paul said, "This one thing I do, forgetting the past and looking forward to the future. I press forward to reach the end of the race to receive the prize for which God, through Christ Jesus, is calling me up to heaven" (Philippians 3:13–14 NIV).

You are in the race of life, not a sprint but a marathon journey, with our Lord Jesus Christ. Though you stumble along the way, Jesus will be there to help you up. If you want victorious living, you must forgive others. Unforgiveness holds you in bondage; your prayers are not answered, you are miserable to be around people you have not forgiven, and God sends tormenting spirits to torment you until you forgive.

Right thinking will bring you victorious living. The Bible says, "As a man thinks, so he becomes" (Proverbs 23:7 NKJV). We become what we think. If you think success, you get success. If you think defeat, you get defeat. Think about the good things that are in your life; make a list and refer to them from time to time. Good people enjoy the positive results of their word (Proverbs 13:21 NLT).

Meditate on the word of God. Renew your mind by reading and meditating on the word of God and the promises he has in store for you.

Jesus will never reject those who belong to him, so you can rest and be glad. Stay plugged into Jesus, for he is your source for God's blessings in your life. Remember that it takes time and maturity before you are able to handle the blessings that God has in store for you. Thank God, who gives us victory over sin and eternal death through Jesus Christ our Lord (1 Corinthians 15:57 NLT).

Spend time with God, read the Bible, and apply the word of God to your life. Seek the Kingdom of God, and he will give you the desires of your heart. Jesus promises peace: I am leaving you with a gift: peace of mind and heart. And the peace I give isn't like the peace the world gives. So don't be troubled or afraid (John 14:27 NLT). Therefore, since we have been made right in God's sight by faith, we have peace with God because of what Jesus Christ our Lord had done for us (Romans 5:1 NLT). He was beaten that we might have peace (Isaiah 53:12 NLT).

Peace is evidence of the Holy Spirit working in your life (Galatians 5:22 NLT). Don't worry about anything; instead, pray about everything. Tell God what you need, and thank him for all he has done. If you do this, you will experience God's peace, which is for more wonderful than the human mind can understand. His peace will guard your heart and mind as you live in Christ Jesus (Philippians 4:6–7 NLT). The Lord gives strength to his people; the Lord blesses his people with peace (Psalm 29:11).You will keep in perfect peace all who trust in you, whose thoughts are fixed on you (Isaiah 26:3 NLT). I have told you these things, so that in me you may have peace (John 16:33 NLT). Let the peace of Christ rule in your hearts, since as members of one body you were called to peace. And be thankful (Colossians 3:15 NLT). The mind controlled by the Spirit is life and peace (Romans 8:6 NLT). Pray often and give thanks to God. Put on the armor of God so you will be ready for the enemy's attack. Be a generous giver, and God will reward you.

Malachi chapter 3 says, "'Bring all the tithes into the storehouse in my temple. If you do,' says the Lord almighty, 'I will open the windows of heaven for you. I will pour out a blessing so great you can't have enough room to take it in! Try it! Let me prove it to you'" (Malachi 3:10 NLT). God will protect your resources; the 90 percent you keep will be blessed way beyond the 10 percent you give by tithing. There are many worthy ministries out there that you can support. I particularly support those ministries who help advance the kingdom of God. Remember: You are investing in the Kingdom of God, and you will have a good return.

The godly love to give (Proverbs 21:25 NLT): If you have money, share it generously. Whoever gives to the poor will lack nothing (Proverbs 28:27 NLT). Honor the Lord with wealth (Proverbs 3:9 NLT). The generous prosper and are satisfied (Proverbs 11:25 NLT). If you help the poor, you are lending to the Lord, and he will repay you (Proverbs 19:17 NLT).

CHAPTER 22

Conclusion

N ow that spiritual truths have been revealed to you, it is time to put them into practice. Adam had authority over all things of the earth while he was in the Garden of Eden. He was given the task of naming all animals and plants. There was no sin in him, so he had an intimate relationship with God. God would speak to him face to face. He had all the provisions he needed in the garden: food, health, a wife, and a long life ahead of him. But when he ate the forbidden fruit, he sinned and was banished from the presence of God and was kicked out of the Garden of Eden. Adam lost his authority over the earth, and the devil took it.

The devil is known as the prince of the air and this world, and now he has the authority that Adam once had.

Jesus came into the world to take back the authority from the devil that he stole from Adam. Jesus has given us authority over the power of the devil. It is high time we use that authority over the enemy and take back what he stole;

it may be your health, finances, or broken relationships. We have the victory through our Lord Jesus Christ.

There is no other name greater in heaven or earth than the name of Jesus. Jesus gave us permission to use his name to defeat the enemy. Our prayers should be offered in his name. In Jesus's name, you can be healed of addictions, strongholds, sickness, and disease, according to his will. You may ask Jesus for anything in his name, and he will do it (John 14:14 NIV).

God's plan for living is simple: put your faith in God and his Son, Jesus. Love God above all else and do his will. If you do this, you will have a blessed life with peace, love, joy, and hope.

COMMENTS

I f you have found this book to be a blessing, share it with others. Purchase this book for friends and family members; it may be the only way for them to know Jesus and get to heaven.

Pray for them that the Lord would lift the veil off their eyes and minds and give them revelation and enlightenment, so they can see and understand the truth of the gospel of Jesus Christ.

Pray for the Holy Spirit to draw them to Jesus. Pray for godly people to witness to them. Pray to take down strongholds: temptations, thought patterns, opinions on religion, materialism, and fear. In the name of Jesus, bind Satan from taking them captive and all wicked thoughts and lies he would try to place in their minds.

Pray that the power of God would be released on them. Declare victory over the devil in their lives. Pray for protection from the enemy's attacks.

You have the authority to petition God for the souls of your friends and family.

May God bless you in all you do, especially for interceding for those you love.

RECOMMENDED READINGS AND OTHER SOURCES

Books

The NLT Indexed Bible
Bible Promises for You www.inspiregifts.com
Battlefield of the Mind by Joyce Meyers
Change Your Word, Change Your Life by Joyce Meyer
How to Win Friends and Influence People by Dale Carnegie
The Power of Positive Thinking by Norman Vincent Peale

Various Teaching CDs

Joel Osteen
Joyce Meyer
Listen to the Positive Preaching of Joel Osteen on Sirius XM
Radio Channel 128

Praise and Worship Music

"So Close to You" by Kent Henry
"You Are My World" by Hillsong Music Australia
"Winds of Worship" by Vineyard Music

Printed in the United States
By Bookmasters